Healing Your Heart:

A guided journal for those experiencing relationship loss after a breakup, separation, or divorce

by

Michelle Post, MA

Licensed Marriage and Family Therapist

Healing Your Heart: A guided journal for those experiencing relationship loss after a breakup, separation, or divorce.
Copyright © 2019, Michelle Post, MA, LMFT
Published and distributed by Post International Inc.
Michelle@PostInternationalinc.com, www.PostInternationalinc.com
All rights reserved. Printed in the United States of America.
No part of this book may be reproduced without permission from the author/publisher.
United States Copyright Office Registration Number TXu-2-155-328
Cover art by anonymous teen

ISBN: 978-1-7331086-0-7 -52495
eBook ISBN: 978-1-7331086-1-4 -50399

Thanks and Dedications:
To the clients who may find some support in completing these pages;

To my clients, friends, and colleagues who inspired me with
their resiliency despite their own broken hearts;

To my two "Bills" — J. William Worden, Ph.D. and Dr. Bill Hoy, D. Min. for their brilliance, compassion, senses of humor, and mentoring all these years. Their collective wisdom has taught me more in 14 years than I could hope to learn in a lifetime.

And to my friends, family and extended family who, in the face of their own losses and changes showed honesty, integrity, sadness, anger, happiness, relief, shock, faith and courage, sometimes all at once.

Preface & Guidance:

"I'm in need of some 911 intervention," she said to me, "My heart is broken … a relationship heart-attack of sorts has killed my spirit. I cannot recover in the same old ways … 'numbing out' with work, food, alcohol, drugs, sex, shopping, replacing the loss with more loss. This time, I want to try something new. I need a way to sort through my pain, my grief, and the death of this relationship."

Interviews from 100+ clients left to pick up pieces after a break-up created a revelation for my work as a Marriage & Family Therapist and for my own healing as I learned to cope with my own life after a heart-breaking divorce. It is estimated that by the time a person "walks down the aisle" for the first time, they have had at least six heart-breaking experiences — none of which have been processed to the point of "healing." Yet, society wonders why the divorce rate is so high. This book of revelation speaks not of the lion and the lamb or trumpets sounding, but of a metamorphosis needed in our world for people to be ready to love again.

As someone once taught me, "Time does not heal. It's what you do with that time that heals".

For me and for all of us who need a heart healer, I have created these pages to help you express your thoughts, your feelings, your reactions, and your memories of a relationship that has left your heart in need of healing. As you go through this book, see which pages interest you now. This book is not designed to be completed all at once or in any special order. In healing after a relationship loss, there is no right or wrong way to feel, think, or react at any given time. I hope that these pages will help you cope as you move along your journey and begin to find healing, and eventually, love again.

~Michelle
Michelle@PostInternationalinc.com
www.PostInternationalinc.com
Facebook: Postinternationalinc
Instagram: @Postinternationalinc
Twitter: @PostInternatio1

First Things First: The Who, How, Where, When, What

My heart has been left in need of healing from my relationship with ...

_____
(name of your partner)

Place a picture of this person (with or without you) on this page.
I invite you to decorate the page and describe the photo and/or when it was taken.
Studies on how to heal from chronic pain have examined brain activity using PET/CAT scans, and have found that the same part of your brain that lights up when you are healing from physical injury is the same part of your brain that lights up when you are engaged in something creative, (e.g., scrapbooking, writing, drawing, knitting, designing, etc.).
Consider delving into a creative hobby or beginning to journal or write music, poems, or songs as your heart heals.

We Met...

Describe how, where, and when you met and a bit about how your romantic relationship began.

10 Things That Attracted Me to...

Think back to the beginning of your relationship and describe some of your partner's characteristics that attracted you to him/her. Who was he/she? What was your partner passionate about and how did you think you were compatible? Feel free to list more than 10, but it's important to identify your own patterns of attraction.

_____

_____

_____

_____

_____

_____

_____

_____

_____

_____

_____

_____

_____

_____

We Dated...

Describe some of your dates, where you went, what you did, and a bit about how your romantic relationship began to develop. Add more information, photos, or draw below.

_____

_____

_____

_____

_____

_____

_____

_____

And then...

Memories

Special Dates in Our Story

My Birthday: _____

My Partner's Birthday: _____

The day we celebrated as our beginning marker/anniversary:
_____

Important other dates to remember...

(Did you get engaged? Move in together? Get married? Add other dates here):

_____

_____

_____

_____

_____

_____

These dates may activate grief reactions as you process through your loss. It may be helpful to plan special days to treat yourself kindly on these dates, go to a spa, hang out with friends, take a trip, do something you enjoy that helps you feel good and supported. See the Healing Exercises section of the book to create a self-care plan.

Our First Kiss...

The magic that encompasses a moment
When you realize you want something more
More than conversation, time spent, friendship
Something that involves chance, prospect, possibility
The Possibility of love, passion, romance
Electrocutes your cells, charges through your body
Commanding attention, alignment, presence, congruence
Imagining, dreaming, hoping, wanting
Wanting something more
All for that one moment
One moment when two people connect
Two lips become one
Two hearts beat fast, full of promise
That one moment when they share a first kiss
I love first kisses
And watching them reminds me of ours.
~Michelle, (May 20, 2003)

Describe your first kiss or some of your first physically intimate experiences.

_____

_____

_____

_____

_____

_____

_____

_____

Pictures and Mementos of Ours

Again, attach some items from your dating life, ticket stubs, photos, etc.

Memories of Special Days and Holidays

Holidays, birthdays and anniversaries can activate relationship grief reactions. Processing the memories can help soften the intensity and prepare you for the days ahead. Write or draw here some details of holidays, birthdays and/or celebrations that you remember spending with the person, include how you felt and/or what you did.

Just Between Us: Letters, Notes, Conversations

Attach some notes, letters, emails, or even write about some key conversations you had as your relationship developed and you began to connect and attach to your partner.

Reminders...

Write, draw, or glue photos of the things that have happened lately that have reminded you of the person: What happened? Where were you? What were you doing? How did you feel?

Things have happened lately that remind me of the person I was in a relationship with. These are ...

Today's date is _____

Reminders I Want...

These are the things I want to do to remember the person I was in a relationship with and the places I want to go to remember the person ...

Write, draw, or glue photos of these things or places.

Today's date is _____

What Happened?

Any Initial Concerns or "Red or Yellow Flags"?

Think back to the beginning of your relationship and describe some of your partner's characteristics or behaviors that may have been initial concerns or "red flags" about your partner or your compatibility with each other. Hindsight is 20/20, as they say, but it's important to tap into your intuition and strengthen your ability to judge character —read the book *Blink* for more about quickly assessing someone.

_____
_____
_____
_____
_____
_____
_____
_____
_____
_____
_____
_____
_____
_____

The Issues?

Describe some of your arguments, disagreements, and signs that things were not going well.
Include your own thoughts, feelings, behaviors, regrets, etc.

_____

_____

_____

_____

_____

_____

_____

_____

_____

_____

_____

_____

_____

_____

What Went Wrong?

Write a poem, or draw symbols or pictures of the factors leading to the downfall of the relationship. For instance, was it infidelity, substance use/abuse/addiction, or other factors that affected the destruction of the relationship? It's important to identify patterns in hindsight to avoid getting blindsided by them in the future or repeating patterns.

The Affair
Sometimes I wonder what goes through your mind when you look at her:
Curvaceous, full-bodied, long sleek neck?
Is your lust for her so overpowering that you can't conceal it, at least in my presence?
I try to compete, to quench your thirst, and leave you satisfied.
Yet, so rarely do you stroke me with that same passion and determination of touch
Or guard me with that same vigilance as you do her.
She is your prize, your confidant, soother and companion.
But let me ask … Is my mouth not so appealing, not as inviting?
Are my juices not as sweet or fulfilling? Is the smell of my breath not as entrancing?
Is my skin not as smooth or as supple? Am I not as worthy of your courting or your pursuit?
You protest, you explain, you beg for pardon.
You say I am more important than she,
Yet you kiss that bottle more than me.
~ Michelle, (November 11, 2000)

The Final Straw?

Many of the people I have worked with describe some moments that felt like the final straw or the nail in the coffin of the relationship. I sometimes refer to these as moments of epiphanies. These epiphanies feel like moments when all of the cells in your body line up and you know you have to act or do something to address what is happening in your relationship. Describe some of your final straw moments as your relationship was ending.

Our Last Encounter

The last time we were together was _____ (day, date)

Describe what happened during this time (e.g., thoughts, feelings, pleasant aspects, regrets). If this was also when the breakup occurred, describe where, when, how it happened, or include this information here as well.

What Next?

The Next Few Days...

Describe what you remember feeling, thinking, doing, reacting, etc. during the first few days after your breakup, separation, or last encounter.

_____

_____

_____

_____

_____

_____

_____

_____

_____

_____

_____

_____

_____

_____

The Next Few Weeks/Months/Years...

What happened over the next few weeks/months/years after the end of the relationship? Include details about how you coped with your first birthday or holiday season after the end of the relationship.

_____
_____
_____
_____
_____
_____
_____
_____
_____
_____
_____
_____
_____
_____

The Changes... The Adjustments

Write about or draw changes and adjustments that your relationship went through in relation to the questions below:

What tasks, things or roles did this person perform, fulfill, or play in your life?

Who could help you do those things or how could you learn to do those things on your own?

Who might help fill those roles in your life for now without replacing that person with another person or without starting to date before your heart is healed?

The People Around Me...

These are the people who supported me and how:

These are the people who were not there for me like I hoped and why:

Today's date is _____

Things People Say/Said...

These are the things people say/said that help me feel supported:

These are the things people say/said that seemed to make my mood or feelings worse:

Today's date is _____

Time of Day...

What time of day seems to be the most challenging for you as you grieve this relationship and adjust to life without this person?

What self-care rituals could you add to this time of day to help you? Write or draw here ...

Processing Sadness...

Write or draw about the things you feel sad about from before or after the end of the relationship.

Before the end of the relationship, I felt sad about these things, events, or people:

Since our relationship ended, I feel sad about these things, events, or people:

Today's date is _____

Processing Anger...

Write or draw about the things you feel angry about from before or after the end of the relationship.

Before the end of the relationship, I remember feeling angry when:

Now, I feel angry about these things, events, and/or people:

Today's date is _____

Who or What I Worry About...

Write or draw about the things you worry about from before or after the end of the relationship.

Before the end of the relationship, I worried about these things, events, or people and this is what I did about my worries:

Since the relationship ended, I worry about these things, events, or people and this is what I do about my worries:

Today's date is _____

What I Miss and Don't Miss About You & Us...

Write or draw about the things you miss most or least about the person and relationship.

What I miss most about you and us being together is:

What I miss least about you and us being together is:

Today's date is _____

Dreams and Wishes

Write or draw about your dreams and wishes.

The dreams and wishes I had for us were.:

The dreams I have had about you (or wish I could have about you) while I slept have been:

Today's date is _____

One Last Day...

Would you want one last day with your partner knowing the relationship still needed to end? If so, write or draw here what you would want to do with your partner to create a positive healing experience. If not, spend some time writing here about what would be too difficult or unwanted about another day together. There is no right or wrong answer here. Just make note that this exercise is not to encourage you to contact the former partner to try to seek this out or share. It is for your own healing, in and of itself.

Changes Over Time

Write, draw or collage here about how you describe yourself, the changes you have been through, and how you think you will be in the future...

PAST

PRESENT

FUTURE

Today's date is _____

Healing Exercises

What Does it Mean to Mourn or Heal?

If mourning is defined as the expression of deep sorrow for someone, then this is how I describe what mourning means to me for this relationship (write, draw, collage):

This is how I describe healing or "healed" (write, draw, collage):

What Helps Me Heal...

Several of the interviewees I spoke with talked of healthy and unhealthy coping mechanisms after their breakup. Unhealthy coping skills were sexual addiction, drugs, alcohol abuse, over-working, over-spending or gambling, over-eating, over-exercise to the point of injury, extended social withdrawal, closing off of the emotions, and/or avoidance of intimate relationships. Healthy coping skills included music, dance, play, going to the park, taking hikes, travel, writing, singing, deepening healthy relationships with friends and/or family, learning new skills or subjects, having fun, walking barefoot in the sand or on wet grass, running through lawn sprinklers, swinging on swings or playing on teeter-totters at the park, gardening, seeing a psychotherapist, reading self-help books, yoga, massage, meditation, prayer, and spiritual development. Keep in mind that too much of anything can interfere with normal daily living.

List the things that help you feel better and schedule time to do the healthy activities several times a week as you heal:

_____

_____

_____

_____

_____

_____

_____

_____

The Relationship Funeral or Memorial

When someone dies, there is a gathering of friends and family, a ritual of sorts to help the grievers bury the deceased and begin the mourning and healing process. This loss ritual is missing when a relationship dies.

Write or draw a memorial service for your relationship:

The Relationship Dash, Defined

It's been said that on a headstone or grave marker, the dash between the date of birth and date of death symbolizes the life lived. Describe what things symbolized or made up the life or dash of your relationship:

___
___
___
___
___
___
___
___
___
___
___
___
___

The Memorial Tablet

If this relationship had a headstone or memorial plaque, I would want anyone who walked by it to read:

My Dash, Defined

Describe your own life's dash. What is the life you want to live and how do you want your life to be described and remembered by others?

_____

_____

_____

_____

_____

_____

_____

_____

_____

_____

_____

_____

_____

Emotions

What things/people/places activate different emotions as you heal? Sad, mad, afraid, scared, guilty, relieved, and happy are some examples of feelings to explore:

_____
_____
_____
_____
_____
_____
_____
_____
_____
_____
_____
_____

Regrets or Wishes?

It's important to learn from your own mistakes in order to avoid repeating patterns in the future. What things, events, words, or actions do you regret about your behavior in the relationship?

_____

_____

_____

_____

_____

_____

_____

_____

_____

_____

Responsibility

If you were to look at who or what was responsible for the end of this relationship and assign each person/event a percentage of responsibility for the totality of the relationship, what would that look like? Relationships are complicated and not all black and white. It's important to identify your own responsibility in the ending of the relationship, not just blame others. Make a legend below for this "Responsibility Pie":

☐ _____   ☐ _____

☐ _____   ☐ _____

☐ _____   ☐ _____

☐ _____   ☐ _____

What I Would Want to Say or Do Now

If you could write or talk to your former partner now, what would you want to say or do? (Note, this is not meant to actually encourage you to speak to the person or mail it, this is meant to help you finish unsaid or undone things for your own well being. In many cases, reaching out to the person to share this is not the healthiest or wisest action. But, finishing this for yourself is often very healing.) Write this on a separate paper or try finishing the sentence starters below:

Dear _____,

I will always remember …

I wish I could forget …

I am so mad that …

I try never to let people see …

You might be proud of me because …

I really wish …

It was so funny when we/you …

I miss you most when …

I Am What I THINK!

No one is perfect. But, beating yourself up for mistakes or missteps can keep you stuck. Instead, write a list of positive affirming statements about yourself that you repeat as a daily mantra for the next 30 days. Examples may include the following:

"I love you"
"I see you and hear you"
"This is painful, and I believe in your ability to heal"
"You don't have to be alone anymore, I am always here for you"
"You are beautiful/handsome"
"You deserve to be loved by the partner of your choice"
"I allow myself to learn from this experience and grow"
"I will let myself be happy again"

_____

_____

_____

_____

_____

_____

_____

_____

_____

Playlist for Healing...

Do you find that music is healing or inspiring for you? If so, make a playlist of songs/artists here that lift up your mood or soothe your soul. What would you call the playlist? If you have access to Spotify, YouTube, or the ability to purchase the songs, create a list of at least 30 songs, and listen to them once a day on shuffle while driving or taking a walk and make note of what they inspire you to do for your own growth or healing.

Playlist title:

Songs and what they inspire:

Laughter is the Best Medicine

Age-old wisdom claims that laughter is the best medicine for healing physical or emotional injuries. Make a list of things or people that are funny and fun and move you to laughter. Consider looking up "laughing yoga" on YouTube or hiring an instructor to teach you. List ways to build laughter into your daily, weekly, monthly, and yearly self-care plan.

_____

_____

_____

_____

_____

_____

_____

_____

_____

_____

_____

_____

"I Like to Move It... Move It"

Research shows that physical activity releases biochemical compounds in the brain that lead to both healing and improving mood. List the physical movements you like to engage in (hiking, walking, dancing, yoga, cycling, swimming, etc.). List ways to build physical movement into your daily, weekly, monthly, and yearly self-care plan.

_____

_____

_____

_____

_____

_____

_____

_____

_____

_____

I Am What I Eat

Health literature is teaming with the importance of nutrition on mood and health. For instance, a lack of vitamin D or sunshine is directly correlated with seasonal affective disorder (SAD). Too much sugar or alcohol is directly linked with mood swings and poor sleep.

Make a list of:

1) Green Light Foods/Beverages that affect your mood for the positive

2) Yellow Light Foods/Beverages that sometimes affect your mood for the worse, but can be enjoyed from time to time

3) Red Light Foods/Beverages that negatively affect your mood or health and need to be avoided most of the time

4) Supplements or actions you can take to aid in your own healing (seek help from a physician or nutritionist for more information or support)

_____

_____

_____

_____

_____

_____

_____

_____

"Show Me the Money"

Many people forget that marriage or living together is also a business relationship. In marriage, for instance, your partner's wealth or debt is also your wealth or debt. When finances are stretched too thin or one is living hand-to-mouth or paycheck to paycheck, this can lead to increased stress and the release of stress hormones. Also, it can lead to poor decisions about relationships. Try some of the following steps to improve your financial health and feel more empowered:

1) Seek a financial planner
2) Make a budget to decrease debt and live within your means
3) Take a financial class, read a financial improvement book, or listen to financial pod casts (Susie Orman and Robert Kiyosaki are two of my favorites)
4) Make some plans to take small or large steps toward your financial goals

Write below thoughts about your partner's attitudes and your attitudes about money, spending, or debt? Finish by setting some goals below for your financial wellbeing:

_____
_____
_____
_____
_____
_____
_____
_____

The Magic of Tidying Up

Marie Kondo was onto something in her book, *The Life Changing Magic of Tidying Up*. A cluttered living space, messy car, or unorganized office is often a reflection of a cluttered mind. What do you need to get rid of? What items from the relationship are you holding on to that bring you sadness verses joy? You may not be ready to rid yourself of all items, and this is totally ok. But, in your mind's eye, are there constant reminders from the relationship that are causing dips in your mood? Do you need to let go of some items or at least store some in a drawer or in the garage? Do you need to:

1) Hire a personal organizer to help
2) Read a book to help you declutter and organize your own items
3) Consider purchasing some items for home or car that bring you joy and need to be added to your space, *for instance, an aromatherapy diffuser
4) Make a list of items that likely need to be moved or stored or given away

Write below what you want to do to improve your living space, car, or office.

_____

_____

_____

_____

_____

_____

_____

_____

Journaling

Start a habit of keeping a daily journal. The research from Pennebaker (University of Texas, Austin) is profoundly powerful about the healing properties of journaling. Start a gratitude journal ... write out five things each day that you are grateful for. Expand as you are able. But, start here. List five things you are grateful for about your life today:

_____

_____

_____

_____

_____

_____

_____

_____

_____

_____

_____

Play and Creativity

When was the last time you built play or child-like activities into your life?
Recreation or play is a vital part of healing. What did you like to do for play as a child?
How can you incorporate more of that into your healing journey?
Go to a park and swing on the swings. Play parachute. Sit outside and blow some bubbles or pick a dandelion and make wishes for your future. Play games with friends.
Get some paints, colored pencils, or crayons and start to color.
Start to draw or doodle right here the ways you plan to incorporate play into your life:

Cinematherapy (Movies and Television)

Film and television can impact personal growth and healing. Watching a movie can activate emotions that need to be released. Quotes can become inspirational mantras or intentions for growth. Have you found movies or television programs that were helpful, healing or inspiring for you? If so, write out the names of movies or TV programs that help you feel good, challenge your growth, or list your favorite inspirational characters or quotes that soothe your soul. Revisit the list below each week. Watch something from this list or review your quotes and journal about the impact on your mood, growth, and healing.

_____

_____

_____

_____

_____

_____

_____

_____

_____

_____

Sleeping

Arianna Huffington wrote a book called *Thrive* and outlined all the current literature about the power of sleep and need to get good rest every night. How are you sleeping? Are you getting at least 7 to 9 hours of sleep each 24-hour period? If not, consider discussing this with your medical physician. Consider trying hypnosis for sleep (YouTube has free options if you search for sleep hypnosis). Develop a sleep hygiene routine including going to bed and waking up at the same time each day, taking a warm shower about 30 minutes before bedtime and/or having a light carbohydrate snack before bedtime. Describe your current sleep pattern below and write some goals here for improving sleep::

_____
_____
_____
_____
_____
_____
_____
_____
_____
_____

Dreaming

Dreams can reveal much about your unconscious and what needs to be processed to help you heal and grow. Often, the meaning of dreams are disguised in symbolism. Keeping a dream journal and seeking professional support for dream interpretation can be a powerful area of healing and growth. List below steps you want to take to address dreams or write out memorable dreams now that you have become aware of the power of dreams:

_____
_____
_____
_____
_____
_____
_____
_____
_____
_____
_____

Sharing is Caring: Volunteerism

In the book called *100 Secrets of Happy People*, the authors cited that people who volunteer report greater life satisfaction than those who do not volunteer. What do you do to help others or give back to your community? What could you do to add some volunteerism into your life? VolunteerMatch.com and Idealist.org are two great sites with many options. List some areas of your volunteer interest here:

_____

_____

_____

_____

_____

_____

_____

_____

_____

_____

Retreat

Do you love nature or travel? When was the last time you spent time alone for a "stay-cation" or went somewhere on a vacation? What calls to you in terms of getting some quiet time or a place to go for retreat? For me personally, I have found incredible healing in Sedona, Arizona or Kauai, Hawaii. Travel feeds my soul. Yet a weekend in my pajamas while writing or reading or taking a hike or walk in the nature around me can be another affordable way to retreat. Also, the act of just planning a trip (even if you don't take it) has been shown to increase the good brain chemistry needed to lift mood. List here some of your ideas for retreat and any steps you can take to plan your next vacation:

*See my retreat and training website www.PostInternationalinc.com for ideas.

_____

_____

_____

_____

_____

_____

_____

_____

You Can and Will Survive This...

If you could look back on the end of the relationship, when (on the date and time) the breakup happened, subtract 5 to 30 minutes before the ending stared and be your own best coach for what was about to come, walk yourself through what is about to happen. Imagine narrating the event to yourself step by step, and then add words of encouragement like, "This is going to be difficult but you will survive this heartache and pain and here is how you are going to survive and heal." Then, outline for yourself the steps you took to help yourself heal. Be encouraging by listing all the learning lessons and by reminding yourself of your strengths of character, your skills, and your self-care plan. Remind yourself of who you were before you met your former partner, what you liked about yourself back then and now. And end with something like, "I believe in you and I love you. You will get through this and learn to live and love again."

Take time to write out some highlights from that coaching, and walk yourself through the process.

Parting Words...

I hope that you have found some helpful support in these pages. This book is not intended to be a replacement for psychotherapy, support groups, or even a good medical check-up, and I encourage you to seek out those supports. Also, I welcome your feedback about this workbook. Like the clients and colleagues who inspired this work, I hope to create new editions as time goes on, as research develops new understanding, and as I hear feedback from people like you who share feedback with me.

As Richard Bach wrote, "What the caterpillar calls the end of the world, the master calls the butterfly".

I hope you find your own metamorphosis.

~Michelle

www.ingramcontent.com/pod-product-compliance
Lightning Source LLC
Chambersburg PA
CBHW042029100526
44587CB00029B/4339